THE ROCK CYCLE

SEDIMENT

John Willis

LIGHTBOX
openlightbox.com

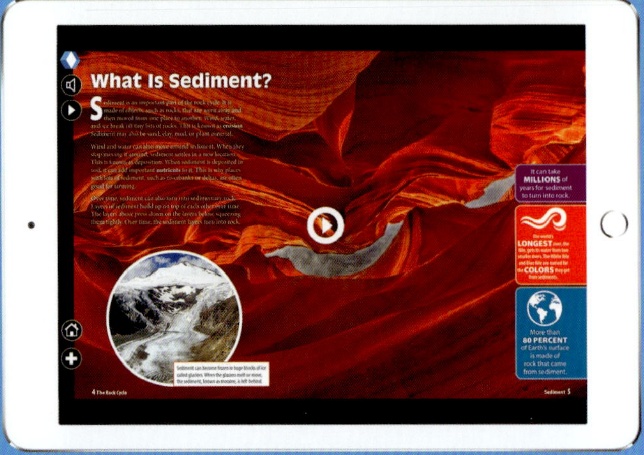

Lightbox is an all-inclusive digital solution for the teaching and learning of curriculum topics in an original, groundbreaking way. Lightbox is based on National Curriculum Standards.

STANDARD FEATURES OF LIGHTBOX

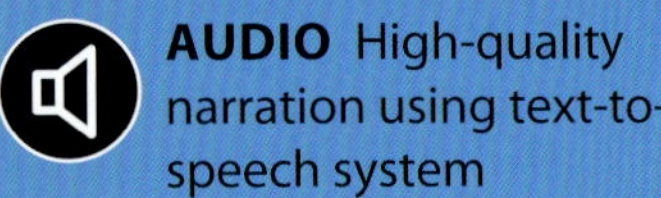
AUDIO High-quality narration using text-to-speech system

ACTIVITIES Printable PDFs that can be emailed and graded

SLIDESHOWS Pictorial overviews of key concepts

VIDEOS Embedded high-definition video clips

WEBLINKS Curated links to external, child-safe resources

TRANSPARENCIES Step-by-step layering of maps, diagrams, charts, and timelines

INTERACTIVE MAPS Interactive maps and aerial satellite imagery

QUIZZES Ten multiple choice questions that are automatically graded and emailed for teacher assessment

KEY WORDS Matching key concepts to their definitions

Contents

What Is Sediment?

Sediment is an important part of the rock cycle. It is made of objects, such as rocks, that are worn away and then moved from one place to another. Wind, water, and ice break off tiny bits of rocks. This is known as **erosion**. Sediment may also be sand, clay, mud, or plant material.

Wind and water can cause sediment to move. Eventually, sediment will settle in a new location. This is known as deposition. When sediment is deposited in **soil**, it can add important **nutrients** to it. This is why places with lots of sediment, such as riverbanks or **deltas**, are often good for farming.

Sediment can also turn into sedimentary rock. Layers of sediment build up on top of each other over time. The layers above press down on the layers below, squeezing them tightly. Eventually, the sediment layers turn into rock.

Sediment can become frozen in huge blocks of ice called glaciers. When the glaciers melt or move, the sediment, known as moraine, is left behind.

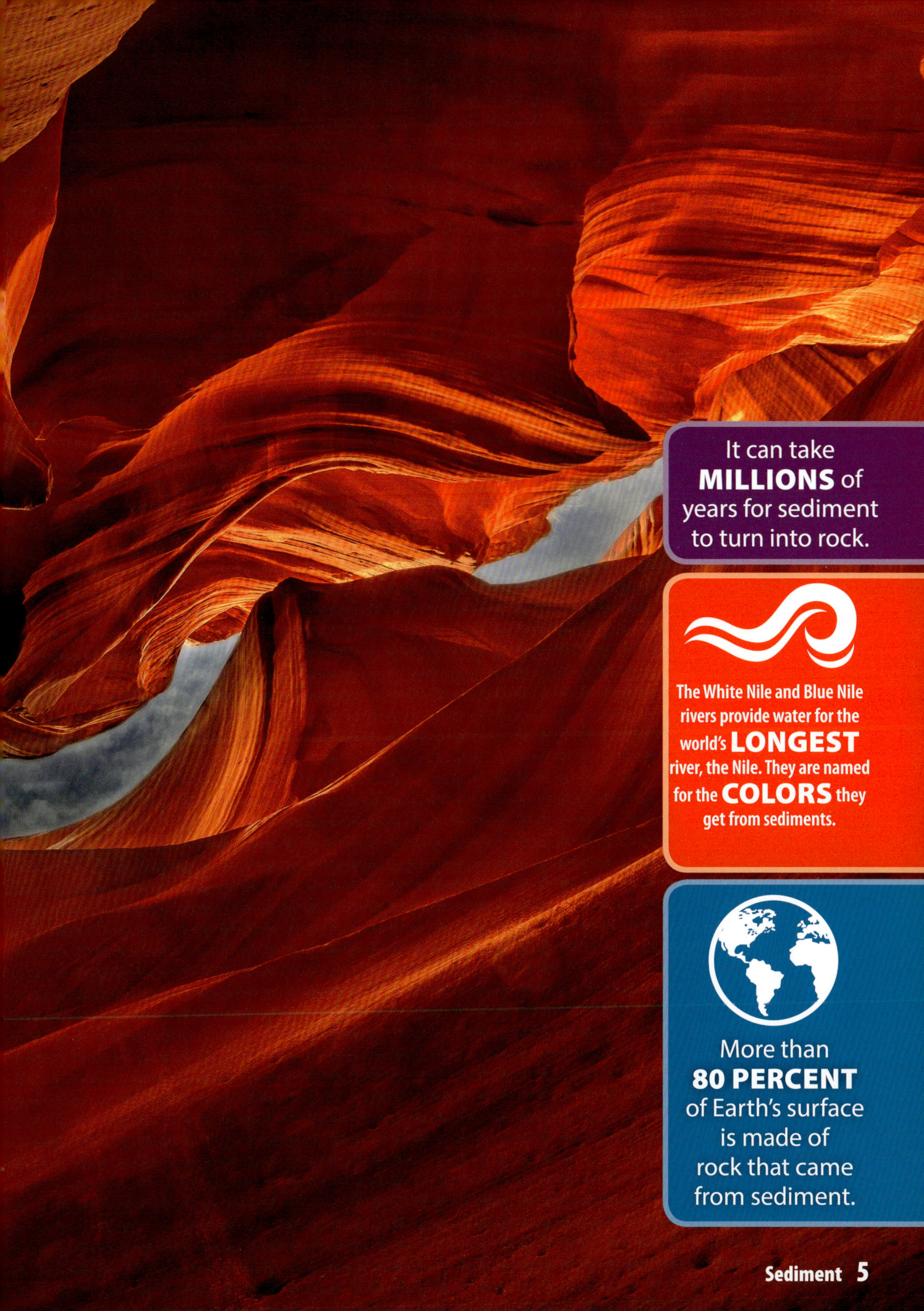

It can take **MILLIONS** of years for sediment to turn into rock.

The White Nile and Blue Nile rivers provide water for the world's **LONGEST** river, the Nile. They are named for the **COLORS** they get from sediments.

More than **80 PERCENT** of Earth's surface is made of rock that came from sediment.

Types of Sediment

Many different materials can make up sediment. However, all sediment is sorted into three main types. Sediment can be clastic, chemical, or biochemical.

Clastic sediment comes from rocks and **minerals**. These objects break down into small pieces called clasts. Sand and clay are examples of clastic sediment.

Chemical sediments are left behind when water **evaporates**. When these sediments turn into rocks, they often form crystals. Chemical sediments include salt and iron oxide, or rust.

Biochemical sediments are also known as organic sediments. They come from living things, such as animals and plants. Peat and shells are both biochemical sediments.

CLASTIC

SAND

- made of pieces of rock, mineral, or soil up to 0.08 inches (2 millimeters) in diameter
- broken into small pieces by wind or rain
- can turn into sandstone in combination with **silt**, clay, and other rocks

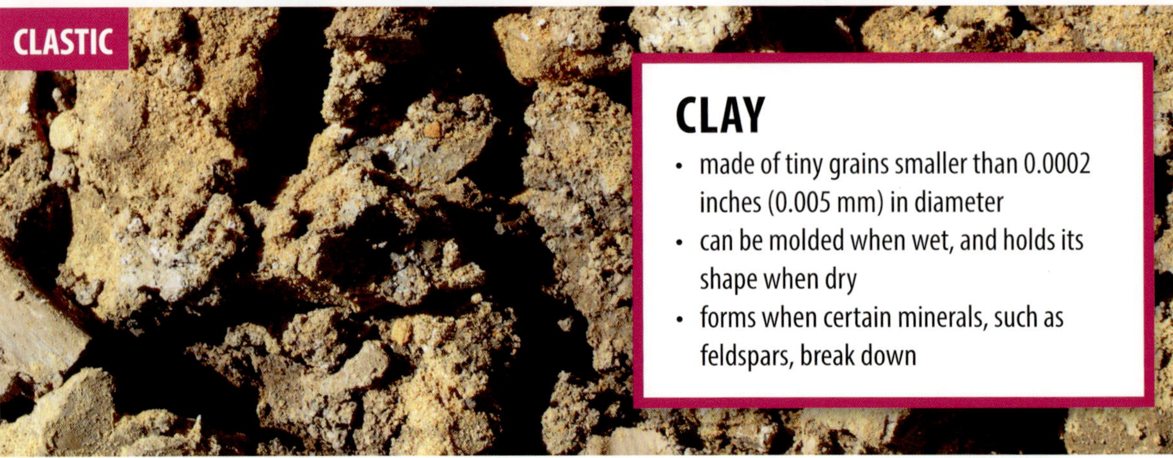

CLASTIC

CLAY

- made of tiny grains smaller than 0.0002 inches (0.005 mm) in diameter
- can be molded when wet, and holds its shape when dry
- forms when certain minerals, such as feldspars, break down

CHEMICAL

SALT

- forms in oceans and other bodies of salt water
- made from sodium, which reaches oceans from rivers, and chloride, which comes from underwater volcanoes
- forms the mineral halite, or rock salt, when water evaporates

CHEMICAL

IRON OXIDE

- formed from iron, one of the most common elements on Earth
- formed when water and oxygen come into contact with iron
- much weaker than iron, and will crumble and be moved when exposed to wind or water

BIOCHEMICAL

PEAT

- found in acidic **wetlands** known as bogs
- formed when plants die but are stopped from breaking down fully by the acid
- a thick, spongy material that can be used for fuel
- if put under pressure, can turn into coal after many years

BIOCHEMICAL

SHELLS

- part of the bodies of animals, made from materials such as calcium carbonate
- when the animal dies, wind or water breaks down and carries hard parts of its body
- can turn into rocks such as limestone

Sediment and the Rock Cycle

The rock cycle is a slow process that recycles rocks. The material that makes up rocks is not destroyed. Instead, it changes from one type of rock to another. The rocks have changed, but the materials they are made from have not. The rock cycle moves very slowly. It can take millions of years for one bit of rock to move all the way through the rock cycle. Rocks break down into sediments over time as part of the cycle. The rocks on Earth today are made from the same material as the rocks on Earth when dinosaurs lived.

Igneous, sedimentary, and metamorphic rocks are the three types of rock that can be created during the rock cycle. Any of these rocks can be broken down by **weathering**, forming sediment. However, weathering is only one way rocks can be broken down. Another way is erosion. This process has created landforms all over the world, including the Grand Canyon.

The Colorado River flows through the lowest part of the Grand Canyon. It cuts into the canyon's rock. It erodes rock on the sides and bottom of the canyon. As the rock wears away, the water level in the river drops and continues to erode layers of newly-exposed rock at the bottom of the river. This process of erosion started about 17 million years ago and continues today. The rock eroded by the river is washed downstream as sediment.

The Grand Canyon is more than 1 mile (1,600 meters) deep at its deepest point.

HOW THE ROCK CYCLE WORKS

Over time, all types of rocks break apart and become sediments. Weathering and erosion cause them to gather and pile up. Pressure pushes the sediments together. This creates sedimentary rock.

High temperature and pressure cause rock to melt. When melted rock cools, it forms igneous rock. Heat and pressure also change sedimentary and igneous rocks into new rocks, called metamorphic rocks. Over time, these new rocks break down into sediment once again.

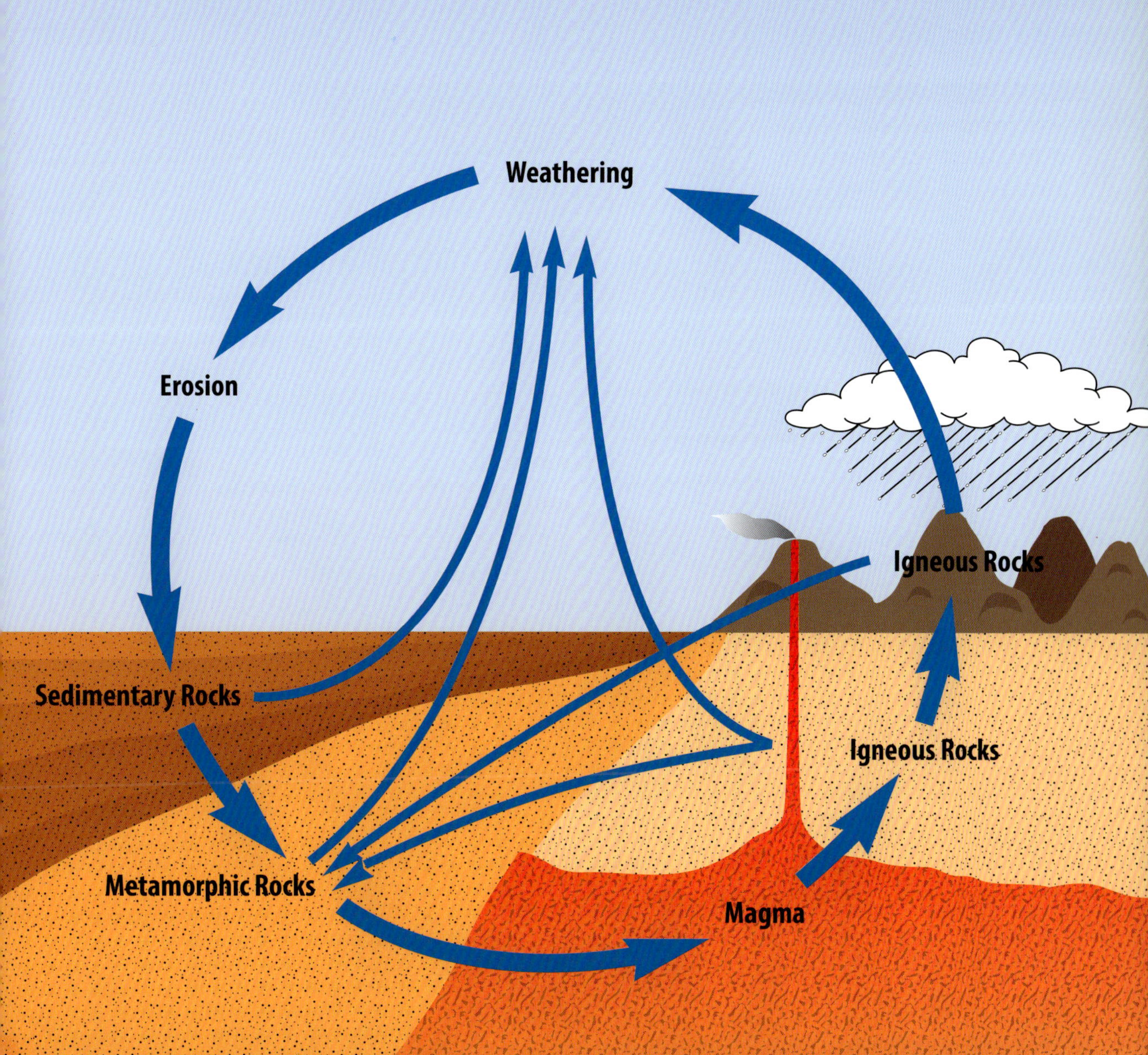

Forming Rocks

Sediment can turn into sedimentary rock in different ways. How the rock forms depends on the materials involved and where it forms. It also depends on the forces acting on the sediment. There are three types of sedimentary rocks. They are known as clastic, organic, and chemical sedimentary rocks. The type of sediment that forms a rock determines which kind it will be.

Uluru, in Australia, is made of a clastic sedimentary rock called sandstone. It formed about 500 million years ago.

Clastic sedimentary rocks form from clastic sediments. These sediments settle and build up in layers. The weight of the upper layers presses down on the lower layers. After many years, the sediment becomes so tightly packed that it turns into rock.

Organic sedimentary rocks form from animal or plant body parts that do not **decay**. This often happens in water with very little oxygen. Other sediments cover the organic material, adding pressure. Over time, the organic sediment is compressed and heated until it becomes a rock such as coal.

Most chemical sedimentary rocks come from chemical sediments that are **dissolved** in water. When the water evaporates, the sediments inside it are left behind. Over time, these materials harden into rock. These kinds of rocks are often called evaporites.

The **OLDEST** known sedimentary rocks on Earth are in Greenland. They are **3.9 BILLION** years old.

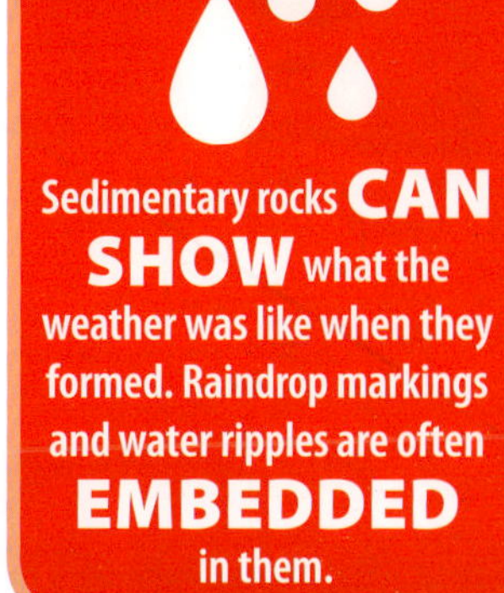

Sedimentary rocks **CAN SHOW** what the weather was like when they formed. Raindrop markings and water ripples are often **EMBEDDED** in them.

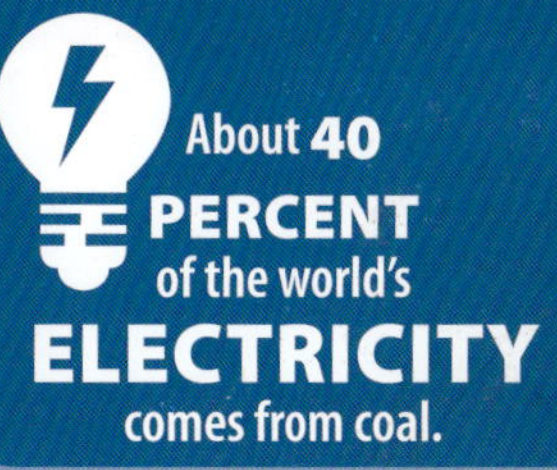

About **40 PERCENT** of the world's **ELECTRICITY** comes from coal.

Fossils

Most animals and plants do not become **fossils** when they die. Many of their bodies decay, or rot. Scavengers eat others. However, if the plant or animal remains do not rot and are not eaten, they can become fossils. Sediment plays an important role in the formation of many types of fossils.

FORMING A FOSSIL

Many of the fossils that **paleontologists** have discovered were created because of sediments.

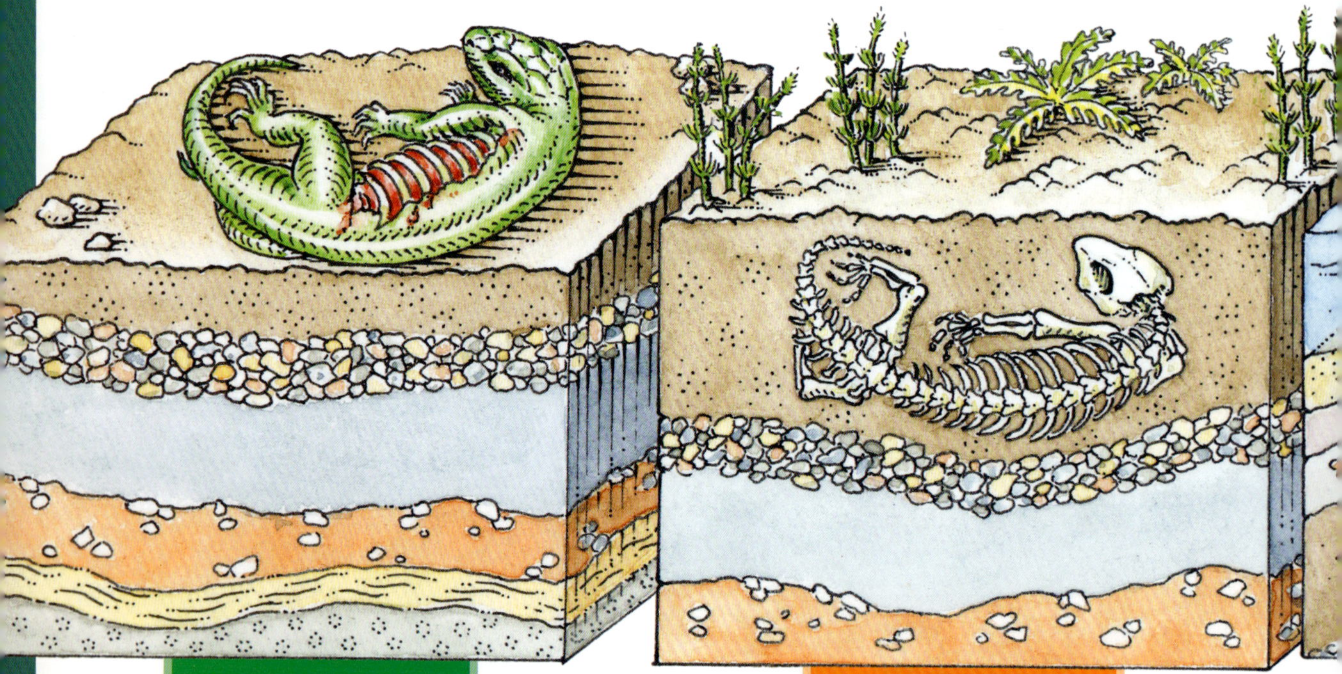

1 An animal dies in a place that scavengers cannot reach.

2 Sediment covers the body. Sometimes, this happens gradually. Other times, floods full of sediment wash over the body. They cover it in a thick layer of dirt, rock, and other material.

A plant or the body of a dead animal can become covered by sediments such as mud or sand. Over time, the weight of the sediment puts pressure on the hardest parts of the body, such as bones, teeth, and shells. They harden into rock. This is called petrification. After thousands of years, these parts become fossils.

Sometimes, a body completely wears away instead of turning to rock. This leaves behind a gap in the rock, which can be filled by sediments. The new sediments take on the shape of the original animal. These fossils are known as cast fossils.

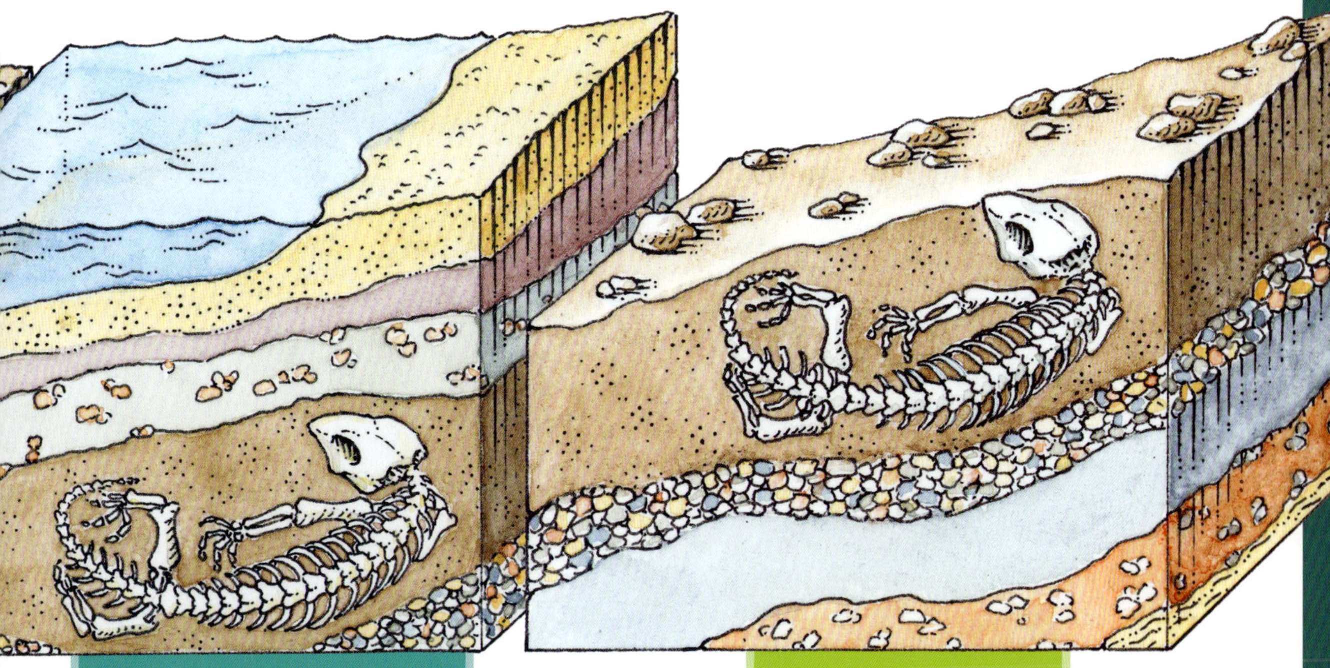

3 Over millions of years, more layers of sediment pile up on top of the body. Parts of the body decay, including spaces within the bones. Minerals enter these spaces and harden. They gradually replace parts of the body. These parts become as hard as stone.

4 Earth's surface moves, splitting the sediment layers. The body, now a fossil, is exposed to view.

Fossils around the World

While fossils can only form under the right conditions, they have been found all over the world. Fossils in sedimentary rock help scientists determine what the climate, living things, and environments were like millions of years in the past.

Name: Lance Formation
Location: United States

The Lance Formation is made of the sedimentary rocks lignite, shale, and sandstone. It is home to some of the best-known dinosaur fossils in the world, including *Triceratops, Tyrannosaurus rex,* and *Ankylosaurus.*

NORTH AMERICA

Atlantic Ocean

SOUTH AMERICA

Pacific Ocean

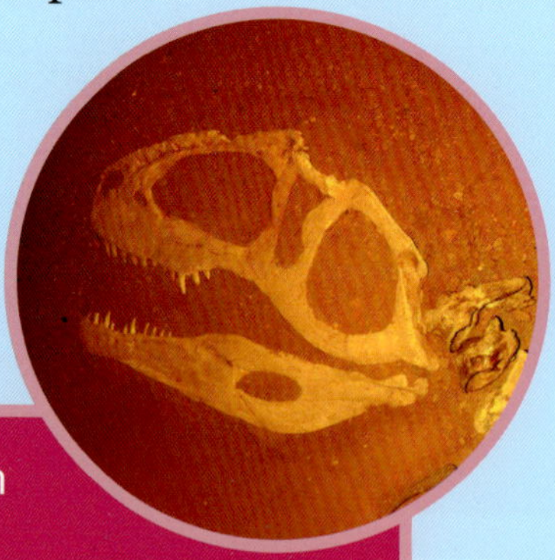

Name: Villa El Chocón
Location: Argentina

The fossil of a *Giganotosaurus*, a large predatory dinosaur, was found in this village in the Argentinian province of Neuquén. Now known for its dry climate, the area was once humid and filled with lakes.

Southern Ocean

Name: Zigong Dinosaur Museum
Location: China

The region of China known as Sichuan is a river valley. Millions of years ago, many dinosaurs in the area were washed downstream when they died. Over time, some rivers dried up, leaving sedimentary rocks filled with fossils. Today, many are on display at the Zigong Dinosaur Museum.

Name: Jurassic Coast
Location: Great Britain

The Jurassic Coast has fossils from many different time periods. Sediment built up over hundreds of millions of years, creating many fossils. Over time, the landscape changed. When the coast eroded, layers of ancient sediment were revealed.

Sediment and Natural Disasters

Sediment can both cause natural disasters and be moved as a result of them. Sediment can build up along rivers. This is more common in areas where plants have been removed. Without plant roots to keep it in place, sediment can easily be moved into a river. Too much sediment can cause a river to rise over its banks. This will cause a flood.

Floods can also speed up erosion and cause sediment to move. In many areas of the world, such as along the Nile River in Egypt, farmers have depended on these sediments to make the soil healthy. However, in many places, floods move large amounts of unwanted sediment. Fields of crops may be covered and ruined. If too much sediment ends up in a river after a flood, animals such as fish may die.

Large amounts of rain can also cause mudslides to occur. In these disasters, the ground becomes **unstable** and moves like liquid. Large amounts of mud and other sediment can move downhill at high speeds. Mudslides are responsible for between 25 and 50 deaths in the United States every year.

Due to the life-giving sediment left behind after its annual floods, ancient Egyptians believed all life came from the Nile.

FLOODING IN THE MIDWESTERN UNITED STATES

In early 2019, large floods took place across the midwestern United States. They were caused after large amounts of rain fell and snow melted on **saturated** soil. Several states declared emergencies as rivers, including the Missouri and the Mississippi, spilled over their banks and flooded.

One of the major effects of the flood was the loss of huge numbers of crops and livestock. More than $1 billion worth of animals and plants, such as wheat and soy, were lost. Many of the crops were covered by the rising waters while in storage. Floodwater carries many kinds of sediments, along with any chemicals that have entered the water. This means that all of the stored grains that were flooded could be **contaminated**. They had to be destroyed in order to make sure no unsafe grains were eaten.

As of May 2019, the wettest recorded period in U.S. history was the time between May 2018 and April 2019.

Sediment Timeline

Many important discoveries have involved sediment. Fossils in sedimentary rock have helped people learn how the world was formed. Sediment has also affected humans throughout history as erosion and floods change Earth's landscape.

3800 BC

Egyptians monitor flow rates of the Nile River. Sediment carried by the river's regular floods keeps the area fertile and healthy.

1027 AD

Avicenna, a scientist living in the area now called Iran, first suggests that liquids carrying sediments might form fossils.

1074

While studying how land forms, Chinese scientist Shen Kuo uncovers marine fossils in areas far from oceans.

Danish scientist Nicolas Steno proposes a theory that sedimentary rocks are layered by age. Layers of sediment are still used to help determine the age of sedimentary rock today.

1669

2000

After reviewing detailed images, scientists determine that Mars has sedimentary rock. This may mean that the planet at one time contained lakes and shallow seas.

2018

California is struck by several large mudslides. Large fires in the area had destroyed many plants that were keeping the soil together. Heavy rain carried large amounts of sediment downhill, causing mudslides which kill 23 people.

Quiz

Now that you have read all about sediment, test your knowledge by answering these questions. All of the information can be found in the text you just read. The answers are provided below for easy reference.

1 What does clastic sediment come from?

4 What can sediment turn into over time?

7 What is another name for biochemical sediments?

10 What are the three types of rock?

ANSWER KEY

1 Rocks and minerals
2 The Colorado River
3 Great Britain's southern coast
4 Sedimentary rock
5 After a body of water dries up
6 Acidic wetlands known as bogs
7 Organic sediments
8 Between 25 and 50
9 *Giganotosaurus*
10 Igneous, sedimentary, and metamorphic

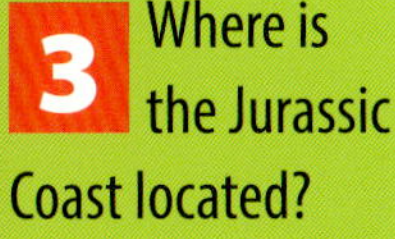

2 What river flows through the Grand Canyon?

3 Where is the Jurassic Coast located?

6 Where is peat often found?

5 When do most chemical sedimentary rocks form?

8 How many people do mudslides kill each year in the United States?

9 Which kind of dinosaur was discovered near Villa El Chocón?

Sediment Layers

Follow these instructions to see how layers of sediment settle.

BEFORE YOU START, YOU WILL NEED

1. Remove any labels from the bottle. Remove the cap.
2. Using the scoop, add equal amounts of sand, gravel, and both kinds of soil to the bottle. Be sure not to fill the bottle completely.
3. Slowly add water to the bottle. Stop when the water is about 1 inch (2.5 centimeters) above the surface of the material.
4. Put the cap back on the bottle. Shake it thoroughly. Predict where you think each type of sediment will end up.
5. Ask an adult to help cut off the top of the bottle using the scissors, leaving about 1 inch (2.5 cm) of plastic above the top of the water.
6. Place the bottle in a sunny area and wait for it to completely dry.
7. Once dry, use the scissors to cut the bottle and sediment in half from top to bottom. This should create a cross section. Using the cross section, determine if your predictions were correct.

Key Words

contaminated: made unfit for use by the addition of something unclean or unwanted

decay: the rotting of organic material

deltas: pieces of land formed by sediments at the mouths of rivers

dissolved: mixed in with a liquid such as water

erosion: the process of being worn away over time and moved, usually by wind or water

evaporates: turns from liquid to vapor, as in the change from water to steam

fossils: impressions of living organisms on rocks

minerals: solids that form naturally from materials that were never alive

nutrients: substances that living things need to live and grow

paleontologists: scientists who study fossils

saturated: soaked or filled with a liquid

silt: fine sand, clay, or dirt

soil: tiny pieces of rock that form the top layer of the ground in which plants grow

unstable: unsteady and easily moved from its location

weathering: when rocks are broken down into smaller pieces by rain, ice, or wind without being moved

wetlands: areas in which excess water is filtered and held

Index

LIGHTBOX

SUPPLEMENTARY RESOURCES

Click on the plus icon found in the bottom left corner of each spread to open additional teacher resources.

- Download and print the book's quizzes and activities
- Access curriculum correlations
- Explore additional web applications that enhance the Lightbox experience

LIGHTBOX DIGITAL TITLES

Packed full of integrated media

VIDEOS

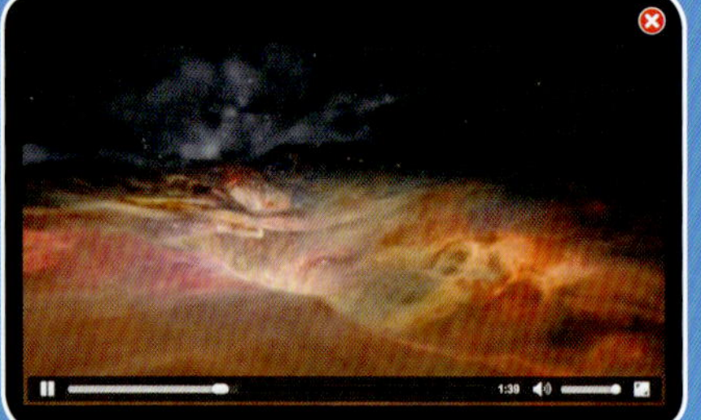

INTERACTIVE MAPS

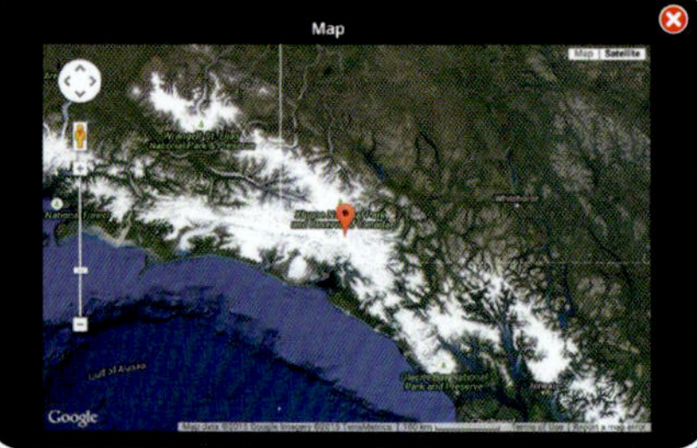

WEBLINKS

SLIDESHOWS

QUIZZES

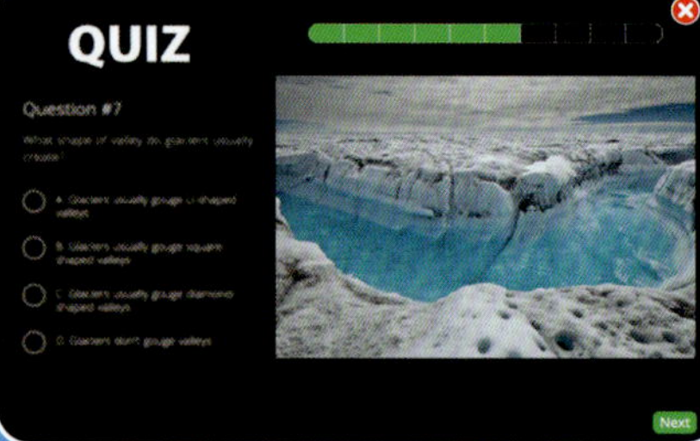

OPTIMIZED FOR

- ✓ TABLETS
- ✓ WHITEBOARDS
- ✓ COMPUTERS
- ✓ AND MUCH MORE!

Published by Smartbook Media Inc.
350 5th Avenue, 59th Floor New York, NY 10118
Website: www.openlightbox.com

Library of Congress Control Number: 2019942190

ISBN 978-1-5105-4443-7 (hardcover)
ISBN 978-1-5105-4444-4 (multi-user eBook)

Printed in Guangzhou, China
1 2 3 4 5 6 7 8 9 0 23 22 21 20 19

072019
122818

Project Coordinator John Willis
Graphic Designer Ana María Vidal

Photo Credits
Every reasonable effort has been made to trace ownership and to obtain permission to reprint copyright material. The publisher would be pleased to have any errors or omissions brought to its attention so that it may be corrected in subsequent printings. The publisher acknowledges Alamy, Getty Images, iStock, Minden Pictures, Newscom, and Wikimedia as its primary image suppliers for this title.